The History of Glendalough, Ireland

DJ Moloney

With Additions by John Hewes

Copyright © 2011 John Hewes

All rights reserved.

ISBN-10: 1456492454
ISBN-13: 978-1456492458

DEDICATION

Dedicated to St. Kevin, founder of the Glendalough religious community. May His spirit abide and his influence continue for generations yet to come.

JH/2010

CONTENTS

1	Glendalough: History of the Vale	1
2	The Gateway	2
3	The Cathedral	3
4	St Kevin's Cross	5
5	The Round Tower	6
6	The Priest's House	10
7	St Kevin's Kitchen	11
8	St Kieran's Church	14
9	The Deer Stone	15
10	The Lakes	17
11	Rhefert Church	20
12	St Kevin's Cell	22
13	St Kevin's Bed	23
14	Tempul Na Skellig	24
15	Our Lady's Church	25
16	St Savior's Priory or the Monastery	29
17	Glendassan	32
18	Life of St Kevin	33
19	Poetry	36
**	Appendix A	41
**	Appendix B	44

ACKNOWLEDGMENTS

Thanks to those individuals and organizations who graciously contributed images for use in this work. A picture can indeed be worth a thousand words, and in the case of Glendalough, so much more.

Image i: Irish Airmail Stamp 1948-1965

FOREWORD

In the following survey I have tried to place the different items of interest in rotation. Starting at the Old Gateway, I have kept the churches as near as possible together. This little book is chiefly compiled for the use of day tourists who have not much time at their disposal, and would like to see and know all the chief interesting features of the glen. I would advise tourists who have at their disposal, and would wish to go more deeply into the architecture of the ruins, to procure the book issued by the Board of Works, which may be had at St. Kevin's Kitchen.

May 1st, 1919   D.J.M.

PREFACE

The original text in this work was published in 1929, in Ireland. My attempt in creating a new version of Moloney's work is to preserve his antiquarian Irish prose style of writing (with minor grammatical enhancements), while at the same time, enhancing the reading experience with the addition of images (most post-date the original text). A bibliography to encourage further reading, as well as other relevant information concerning Glendalough, Ireland and Irish monks, completes the work.

July 1, 2010   JH

1 GLENDALOUGH: HISTORY OF THE VALE

So Irish monks went forth from the monasteries (then in large numbers in the country) to preach and revive learning and religion. Glendalough contributed a large number of monks for this purpose, and even to the present day the ruins of their monasteries can be seen dotted over the Continent.

Image 1: Glendalough Circa 1900

Glendalough is reached after a delightful drive through the Vale of Clara (through which the Avonmore flows to meet the Avonbeg at the Vale of Avoca) from Rathdrum, or by a much longer route through the Devil's Glen and Roundwood from Rathnew. Unfortunately, the stay of the tourist travelling by the latter route is too short to appreciate to the full the beauty and ancient ruins of the glen; in fact, any day journey will not show the tourist all the ruins of the famous Seven Churches.

Approaching the valley from either Rathdrum or Rathnew, the old Gateway which led into the ancient "city" is the first ruin reached.

2 THE GATEWAY

This gateway, the only one of its kind surviving now, in Ireland, led into the ancient "City of Glendalough" It consists of two unornamented arches of an early date, measuring 9 feet 3 inches in width and 2 feet 6 inches in thickness. The walls enclose a space of 16 feet in width and 16 feet 5 inches in length. The floor is paved with rough stones and gradually sloped upward towards the graveyard. Just outside the second arch a crude cross with gradually expanding ends is cut in a rectangular slab of mica slate.

The arches are said to have been surmounted by a tower of the same type as the Round Tower now in existence, but not quite so high. But there may have been only another storey or guardroom, as the foundation is not sufficiently strong to bear a very high one. This room was used by sentries, who always kept watch at such places. The ground is elevated at the eastern wall, so access to the upper chamber may have been by a door.

Image 2 The Gateway

Passing through the gateway, the tourist sees the ruins of the largest of the churches, the Cathedral.

3 THE CATHEDRAL

Situated in the centre of the cemetery, this church is the largest of the ruins. The Cathedral, which was dedicated to St. Peter and St. Paul, ceased to be a cathedral in 1214, when the diocese of Glendalough was united to Dublin. The church consists of a nave and chancel, with a vestry or sacristy at the south side. The nave is 48 feet long by 29 feet 5 inches wide, the walls being 3 feet 5 inches thick. The chancel is 37 feet 7 inches long, by 21 feet 9 inches in width, the end walls being 3 feet 6 inches, and the side walls 3 feet thick.

Image 3: Cathedral & Headstones

The masonry indicates many rebuildings ; the lower part consists of large squared stones to the height of from 3 feet 6 inches to 6 feet in places. Above these are small rough stones, intermingled with the rough stones are several mica blocks, which were prepared for, or formed part of another building. One of these blocks has been removed by the Board of Works, and can be seen at St. Kevin's Kitchen. In the west is a fine cyclopean doorway 6 feet 9 inches in height and 3 feet 4 inches to 3 feet 11 inches wide, the sides forming a slight incline. The church is lighted by two windows in the south side 4ft. 6ins. high by 1 foot 6 inches in width externally, gradually expanding to 2 feet internally. A fine specimen of Irish Romanesque is found in the chancel arch. The chancel is of a much later date than the nave, and is 8 feet narrower. The east window, 10 feet 9 inches high, by 1 foot 6 inches wide, was beautifully carved. But many of the stones are missing, and those that remain are much weather-beaten. The vestry doorway from the .chancel is plain. In the vestry itself there are no traces of windows or doorway in the masonry.

Image 4-A: Cathedral Interior

Image 4-B: Cathedral Arch

4 ST. KEVIN'S CROSS

Situated to the south of the Cathedral is St. Kevin's Cross. It is 11 feet 3 inches high by 3 feet 10 inches across the arms, and 1 foot 5 inches wide, and consists of undressed granite.

Beneath this cross the saint is supposed to be buried, but some maintain he is buried in Our Lady's Chapel, which lies to the west of the graveyard.

Image 5-A: St. Kevin's Cross

Image 5-B: St. Kevin's Cross and Scenery

5 THE ROUND TOWER

Image 6: Round Tower

Is situated to the north-east of the Cathedral. It is 110 feet in height, and 52 feet in circumference, at the bottom slightly tapering towards the top, the door being 10 feet from the ground. The date of its construction is unknown, but is believed to have been built at the same time as the Cathedral, namely, the 6th century. Above the ground level, on the inside, are the marks of where beams entered the wall, these holes occur in the walls at different stages higher up, which would indicate the presence of floors. It has few windows except at the top floor, which has four, facing the cardinal points. The origin of those towers is a matter of opinion, some maintain they were used as watch towers and bell towers ; while others say they were used as places of refuge for storing the sacred treasure of the churches in time of attack. The latter theory seems most feasible, as they are always found near old churches and monasteries, the door being always far from the ground.

The door in this tower faces the south-east, and is constructed of dressed granite without ornamentation. The jambs, which are slightly inclined, measure 5 feet 8 inches in height, by 2 feet wide at the sill, and 1 foot 9 inches at the head. The top was destroyed by lightning, but was rebuilt in 1876 by the Board of Works with the original stones found in the debris inside; a lightning conductor has since been installed.

THE HISTORY OF GLENDALOUGH

Image 7-A: Round Tower Seen Through Window

Image 7-B: Round Tower & Cemetery

Image 8-A Round Tower & Ruins

Image 8-B Historical Image from 1841

THE HISTORY OF GLENDALOUGH

Image 9-A: Round Tower & Cemetery

Image 9-B St Kevin's Kitchen & Round Tower

6 THE PRIEST'S HOUSE

Situated to the south of the Cathedral. This structure was built some time about the 12th century. It was a total wreck fifty years ago; but was rebuilt by the Board of Works from drawings of the original. Inside are buried some of the priests of the parish. The east wall and window are beautifully carved on the outside, but many of the original stones are missing. The inside dimensions are 14 feet 8 inches long by 7 feet 9 inches wide. There is a recess in the west wall 2 feet 5 inches wide, locally known as the "Wishing Stone," and a narrow doorway 5 feet 10 inches by 1 foot 10 inches wide in the south wall. Over the door is a sculptured stone, the top of which has disappeared; three figures are carved thereon, thought by some to represent St. Kevin seated between a bishop with a crosier and a bell-ringer.

    It is too small to be a priest's dwelling; but it may have been used as a library or oratory. The niche in the wall may have been used for the statue of a saint, possibly St. Kevin himself, and into this oratory people went to pray before the statue.

    Leaving this structure, the tourist turns towards the south and sees the belfry and stone roof of St. Kevin's Kitchen quite close to the cemetery.

Image 10 Priest's House & Tombstones

7 ST KEVIN'S KITCHEN

Cro chaeimbghin, or Kevin's house, or Kitchen, is the most interesting structure now remaining at Glendalough. It probably received Kitchen from the dwarf round tower on top, being mistaken for a chimney when covered with ivy.

In this the saint lived for some time after leaving the cave at the lake. Built in 533, it consisted of a nave only 22 feet 8 inches in length, and 14 feet 7 inches in width. At a later date the east wall was pierced and a chancel 10 feet 3 inches by 9 feet 3 inches (not now in existence), and a vestry, still standing, 9 feet 3 inches in length, and 7 feet 8 inches in width, were added. The vestry has an opening window in the eastern side 5 inches wide, with rounded head widely splayed internally.

The small round tower on top was used as a belfry, and was probably built at the same time as the chancel and vestry, as it is of a much later date than the nave. It is 9 feet in height, and has four windows facing the cardinal points like the large tower. There is an upper room or attic 5 feet high by 5 feet in width, which was lighted by a single window on the eastern side. The most remarkable feature of the building is its stone roofs; the stones of which are set horizontally, one against the other, so that they form an arch. The attic between the roofs seems too low for a living room. The theory of some is, i.e., that the inner roof was built to strengthen the outer. The crack in the southern wall extending to the roof is not a defect in the building itself, but was caused by the breaking out of a small window, which then existed in the wall, to enlarge it, by persons who in-tended to use the church for service.

In 1163 Glendalough was burned, and according to the Annals of the Four Masters this church was damaged by fire. Inside the church is a collection of loose fragments of the churches, old crosses and tombs brought in for safety, from the elements and vandalism of some tourists. In the centre is the Market Cross, which stood near the Royal Hotel, that being the Market Square. It is beautifully interlaced on the back and sides with the crucifixion and some nearly obliterated figures in front. Near the walls are the querins, or grinding stones, by which corn was ground. A tombstone with an inscription in Latin and Irish, and a round stone or column already referred to as being in the wall of the Cathedral.

Image 12-A St. Kevin's Kitchen & gate

Image 12-B St. Kevin's Kitchen Rear View

THE HISTORY OF GLENDALOUGH

Image 13-A Side View St. Kevin's Kitchen 1

Image 13-B Distant View St. Kevin's Kitchen

8 ST. KIERAN'S CHURCH

Cro Kieran or St. Kieran's church is situated just outside the turnstile at St. Kevin's Kitchen. This church was unearthed in 1875, when the Board of Works began to restore the churches. It was dedicated by St. Kevin to St. Kieran, the founder of Clonmacnoise. It consists of a nave 18 feet 10 inches in length by 14 feet 6 inches in breadth, and chancel 9 feet 4 inches by 8 feet 10 inches. The work is crude and devoid of ornamentation, denoting its early date. A stone altar is situated at the eastern end, and in the south side are the remains of a door, off the chancel, that may have led to a vestry. Until discovered, its existence was nearly forgotten.

Image 14 Foundation of St. Kieran's Church, to the right of St. Kevin's Church

9 THE DEER STONE

Crossing the bridge further south, the tourist sees a collection of stones. The centre stone with the hollow is called the Deer Stone. This stone is associated with a local legend.

According to the legend, when the churches were being built, one of the men's wives died, leaving two children. So St. Kevin taking pity on the children commanded the deer to come down from the mountain at the back, Derrybawn, to be milked into the hollow stone; on a stone nearby is the mark of where the father sat, and close to it are the marks of his four fingers and thumb.

Image 15 Foot Bridge

Definition of Bullaun Stone, which is the term used to describe the Deer Stone as well as other similar stones found in Ireland and beyond (added by John Hewes, 2011).

A bullaun (Irish: bullán; from a word cognate with 'bowl' and French 'bol') is the term used for the depression in a stone which is often water filled. Natural rounded boulders or pebbles may sit in the bullaun.[1] The size of the bullaun is highly variable and these hemispherical cups hollowed out of a rock may come as singles or multiples with the same rock.[2][3]

Local folklore often attaches religious or magical significance to bullaun stones, such as the belief that the rainwater collecting in a stone's hollow has healing properties.[4] Ritual use of some bullaun stones continued well into the Christian period and many are found in association with early churches, such as the 'Deer' Stone at Glendalough, County Wicklow.

[Roser1954, et al; Wikipedia, obtained on-line 2/13/2011, used under Creative Commons Attribution-Share Alike License; http://creativecommons.org/licenses/by-sa/3.0/]

10 THE LAKES

Continuing the green road to the right, the tourist soon finds himself at the Lower Lake. This is the smaller of the two, and is 400 yards long by 200 yards in breadth. It is linked to the Upper Lake, and drained by the Glenale River, which takes its rise at the head of the Upper Lake. Passing the Lower Lake, a remarkable cliff is seen to the left in the face of the mountain. This is known as the " Giant's Cut," and is supposed to have been caused by a blow of Finn M`Coul's sword. About half a mile further on the Upper Lake is reached. Situated between Lugduff and Camaderry mountains, it is much larger than the one just passed. It is a little over a mile in length and a quarter mile in breadth. The Glenalo River feeds it at the extreme end and Polanass brook on the southern side. About 100 yards up this brook a splendid waterfall can be seen, especially when the brook is swollen by rain. The lake has a dismal appearance, due to the dark overhanging mountains. In the cliffs at the south side is the famous St. Kevin's Bed, where the saint lived for seven years until discovered by some persons tending sheep. At the end of the Upper Lake white heaps may be noticed; lead mining was carried on there, but owing to the increase in the cost of transport and the decrease in the price of ore, it was abandoned. Extensive veins of lead yet remain in the mountain.

Image 17 Upper Lake of Glendalough

Image 18-A Upper & Lower Lakes

Image 18-B Lower Lake

Image 19-A Walking Trail Along Lake

Image 19-B Stream Along Side Glendalough

11 RHEFERT CHURCH

By crossing the Polonass Brook and turning to the right, the tourist comes upon the ruins of Rhefert Church. The name Rhefert denotes the burial place of the kings. In this church the O'Tooles, who were chiefs of the Wicklow clans, were buried. Their tombstones, however, have disappeared owing to the vandalism of some tourists. A slab marking the tomb of King McMthuil dated 1010 lay near the south wall, but it has disappeared. The church is ideally situated, and is surrounded by a cemetery which contains many old interesting tombs and crosses. The church itself consists of a nave 29 feet in length and 17 feet 3 inches in breadth, and chancel which measures 13 feet by 7 feet 11 inches. The west doorway is 2 feet 8 inches at the base, slightly inclining to 2 feet 6-1/2 inches at the top, being 6 feet 4-1/2 inches in height. The jambs are formed of dressed granite.

The nave is lighted by two small windows in the south wall 2 feet 3 inches in height which have their heads cut out of single stones. The chancel has a single window in the east end 3 feet in height and 5-3/4 inches wide expanding internally to 18 inches. There is a small recess in the wall near the chancel arch. The chancel arch is unornamented, and consists of dressed granite like the doorway. The resemblance of Rhefert Church to Trinity Church in dimensions and style of building seems to indicate they were both built about the same time. The church itself has been much restored by the Board of Works. On the northern bank of the river opposite Rhefert Church are the remains of what may have been an ecclesiastical building. Its size is uncertain owing to the destruction of the west wall. On the western side a few crude crosses can be seen.

Image 20 Cigarette Box Featuring Rhefert Church

THE HISTORY OF GLENDALOUGH

Image 21-A Rhefert Church & Cemetery

Image 21-B Rhefert Church Interior

Image 21-C Rhefert Church Arch

12 ST. KEVIN'S CELL

Continuing the road at Rhefert Church for a short distance, St. Kevin's Cell is reached. It is situated on a cliff overhanging the lake. Circular in shape, the walls being three feet in thickness, and vary in height from one to three feet. A rough stone cross is in the centre, probably denoting a burial. This must be the hut stated in his life to have been built between the mountain and the lake.

Image 22 Foundation of St. Kevin's Cell

13 ST. KEVIN'S BED

Taking a boat at the northern side of the lake, a quarter of a mile row will bring the tourist to the southern shore under St. Kevin's Bed. A good view of the rock and bed itself can be obtained from the boat before landing. It is situated about 30 feet above the surface of the lake, and is a small cave 4 feet in height and 7 feet in length. In this cave the saint lived for seven years. The people who came to visit him after his discovery by the shepherds built the church, Tempul-na-Skellig, which can be seen close by. Laurence O'Toole as Abbot of Glendalough, and afterwards as Archbishop of Dublin, came to this little cell to spend the Lenten season.

The legend of the drowning of Kathleen, so aptly described by Moore's well-known lyric, is too familiar to require repetition. But there seems to have been some foundation for the legend. According to the Codex Kilkenniensis, a young girl did actually follow St. Kevin. Being displeased with her unsought attentions, he beat her with nettles, whereupon the maiden vowed to live a single life, afterwards becoming one of his disciples.

Image 23 St. Kevin's Bed & Tempul Na Skellig

14 TEMPUL NA SKELLIG

Tempul-na-skellig, or the "Church of the Rock," is situated on the southern shore of the lake, within a short distance of St. Kevin's Bed. It was the first church built in the valley, being built for St. Kevin by the people who flocked to see him after he being discovered in his cave by some shepherds. The church itself is very small, and much defaced from landslides from the mountain. The structure is 26 feet long by 14 feet wide. The walls, with the exception of the northern wall, which measures 3 feet, is 2 feet 6 inches thick.

The west doorway is formed of dressed granite, with inclined jambs. The east window has two lights 2 feet 9 inches by 5-1/2 inches, the heads of which are cut from a single stone. At the back of the church is a wall, probably built to keep the land from sliding on the church below. Outside the church are several plain tombstones and several nicely carved crosses. A short distance from the doorway another flight of steps begins which leads to an artificially made green platform, with a wall built at the mountain side to keep it from falling as before mentioned. Other artificially made green platforms, with a wall built at the mountain slides, have swept away all traces, or they may have been built of wood and were burned, as the presence of a large quantity of charcoal would seem to denote.

Image 24 Pathway to St. Kevin's Bed Circa 1900

14 OUR LADY'S CHURCH

This church is situated to the west of the cemetery, and is best reached by crossing the steps at the Round Tower, and crossing the adjoining field. This church was dedicated to the Blessed Virgin, and is supposed to be the earliest church erected in the lower part of the valley. Some writers maintain the saint himself is buried in this church, but in what part of the enclosure he was interred has not been given. The dimensions of the structure are: The nave, which is the older part, 32 feet in length and 19 feet 11 inches by 19-1/2 feet, like the Cathedral, but not so marked, the masonry is of two periods. The large dressed stone at the bottom and the rougher work above it, being most marked in the east gable. The walls are from 3 feet 2 inches to 3 feet 7 inches in thickness.

The most interesting feature of the building is the west door, which consists of seven stones, all dressed granite. It is 6 feet 7 inches in height, and tapering from 2 feet 11 inches wide at the bottom to 2 feet 6 inches at the top.

The soffit of the lintel has an incised cross circularly expanding at the ends. Only the piers of the chancel arch remain; these are plain, being built of dressed stone. The chancel contains a rough stone altar, in which is fixed a small font. The east window is round headed, and measures 3 feet 3 inches by 11 inches inside, splayed to 3 feet 11 inches, the head being slightly ornamented. In the chancel are two ornamented slabs, one being over the altar. Within the enclosure of the church are many unornamented slabs marking the burial of its former inhabitants.

Image 26-A Our Lady's Church (Center, behind trees)

Image 26-B Brook Running through Glendalough

15 TRINITY CHURCH

Situated by the roadside about a quarter of a mile below the Royal Hotel. This church is in a good state of preservation. Formerly a round tower 60 feet in height, surmounted this structure; but it was blown down by a storm in 1818. A fine old Celtic cross, the head of which is now to be seen in St. Kevin's Kitchen, was broken by its fall.

The church consists of a nave and chancel, the former 29 feet 4 inches in length by 17 feet 6 inches in width; the latter measures 13 feet 6 inches in length by 8 feet 9 inches in breadth. The round tower was of a much later date than the original church, as the door leading into the chamber on the western side was the external doorway before this building was constructed. The round-headed doorway in the southern walls is of a much later period and was constructed when the round tower was built against the western entrance. There is a small window in the south wall of the nave measuring 2 feet 4 inches in height and 8 inches in width, expanding inside to 2 feet. The chancel has two small windows, one in the eastern wall, with a semi-circular head cut from a single stone. The south window consists of two flat stones that meet at the apex of the opening. The chancel arch is plain, and consists of dressed granite; the keystone having slipped a little. There is a marked resemblance between this arch and west door with those of Rhefert Church, as if they were built about the same period.

All the windows in the churches are narrow outside and splayed internally. The reason being, as glass was unknown, a window built in such a manner gave ample light and prevented much rain coming through.

Trinity was founded by a disciple of St. Kevin's, St. Mochuarog. But it received the name Trinity at a much later period.

Image 27 Lion Carving on Trinity Church

Image 28-A Trinity Church

Image 28-B Earlier Doorway, Trinity Church

Image 28-C Newer Doorway, Trinity Church

16 ST SAVIOR'S PRIORY OR THE MONASTERY

This church is reached by crossing the bridge to the south of St. Kevin's Kitchen, inclining to the left, then following the green road until an iron gate is reached, crossing the steps close by, and continuing the green road until another iron gate looking down towards the river is reached; passing through this gate the Monastery can be seen by the river surrounded by fir-deal trees.

This is the latest church built in the valley, and is said to have been founded by St. Laurence O'Toole, afterwards Archbishop of Dublin. The structure consists of a nave (40 feet 11 inches long by 20 feet 7 inches wide), chancel, and at the northern side the remains of a domestic building. The chancel, which was almost all re-erected by the Board of Works, has beautifully ornamented work (especially the chancel arch) belonging to the twelfth century, but many of the stones have been misplaced. The chancel arch is well constructed, measuring 10 feet 4 inches span. The chancel, which is 17 feet 4 inches by 11 feet 6 inches, was formerly covered by an arched roof. The side walls are 4 feet in thickness. The chief item of interest in the chancel is the east window, which is beautifully ornamented. It has two lights with semi-circular heads cut in a single stone 3 feet 10 inches by 9-1/2 inches. Many of the original stones have disappeared.

The apartment to the north is 18 feet 7 inches and 16 feet wide. It has two lights, one in the eastern wall 3 feet 3 inches by 10-1/2 inches, splayed internally to 3 feet 9 inches. The northern window is 3 feet by 8-1/2 inches, splayed to 4 feet 6 inches internally. Under the east window a recess occurs in the wall; in this recess a flight of steps commences through the wall, which must have led to another storey. This church was once the centre of a large religious settlement. The domestic buildings must have been of wood, as no trace remains.

All the loose stones belonging to this church, which were found after its reconstruction, are preserved in St. Kevin's Kitchen.

Image 30-A St. Savior's Interior

Image 30-B St. Savior's Side View

Image 31-A
Ornamentation St. Saviour's Church

Image 31-C St. Savior's Window

Image 31-B St. Savior's Apartment Door

Image 31-D St. Savior's Stairway

17 GLENDASSAN

A few hundred yards below the Royal Hotel a road joins the one from Laragh. This leads to the Vale of Glendassan. In this vale lead mining was carried on, as the white heaps denote. The road leads on towards the Wicklow Gap, through bog on one side and Tonlagee Mountain on the other. The Glendassan River flows down in the valley below, receiving a tributary from Lough Nahanagan, which is situated basin-like near the top of the mountain. This lake is nearly round, being about half a mile in diameter. The river Glendassan flows by the Royal Hotel, meeting the Glenalo from the Glendalough lakes, a few hundred yards further on.

The glen is reached by crossing the bridge at laragh, and inclining to the left. It is a long uninteresting glen, with the Glenmacanns waterfall (which is the only item of interest to be seen therein) at the extreme end. The word Glenmacanass is derived from meacana, a wild tap root and eas a waterfall.

Image 32-A Glenmacanass Waterfall

Image 32-B The Royal Hotel

18 LIFE OF ST. KEVIN

Coemgen, i.e., fair offspring, Kevin, the founder of the great ecclesiastical city of Glendalough, and builder of the Seven Churches, was born in 498 and died at the age of 120 years on 3rd June, 618. According to early chronicles, Kevin was a member of the royal family of Leinster. He received his early education from his uncle, St. Eoghan (Eugene), Bishop of ardstraw, at the monastery of kilnamanagh, near Glenealy. Renouncing worldly ambition after his ordination, the young man retired to the solitude of Glendalough in the early part of the sixth century. In this uninhabitable vale he lived a hermit's life for many years.

At the northern shore of the Upper Lake he made a hollow tree his dwelling; retiring from here after four years to the southern shore, where the cave now known as St. Kevin's Bed sheltered him. After a few years of a lonely life here, he was discovered by some shepherds tending their sheep on the mountains. News of his discovery having been made known, a multitude of people came to visit the holy man. Many remained with him as disciples. They built him a chapel near his cave, now known as Temply-na-skellig. Soon his church became overcrowded with disciples. At this time, as tradition tells, one of the O'Toole chiefs granted the land to St. Kevin on which the Seven Churches were afterwards built. Rhefert Church was then built lower down the valley, and around it a religious settlement sprang up. One by one the other churches were built, and near each a school for learning and a college for religion quickly appeared.

"Around the monastery," says Archdall, "grew up a small city, and a seminary was founded, from which were sent forth many saints and exemplary men, whose sanctity and learning diffused around the western world, that universal light of letters and religion, which in earlier ages shone so resplendent through this, remote, and at the same time tranquil, isle, and were almost exclusively confined to it."

For about five hundred years, till 977, Glendalough was one of the most important ecclesiastical and educational settlements in Ireland. At this time the Danes of Dublin destroyed the city by fire and sword. Five years later the city was sacked again by the foreign marauders, and again in 984 and 985. In 983 the lands were plundered by the native Irish. The city was again burnt by the Danes in 1012 and 1016. In 1163 Cro Caoimhgin, Kevin's House or Kitchen narrowly escaped destruction in a fire which destroyed part of the town. In 1176 it was ravaged by the Anglo-Normans. In 1177 a bridge and mills in the town were swept away by a flood in the river. The crowning disaster occurred in 1398, when the English forces destroyed the city, whereupon it ceased to be inhabited.

The names of two of St. Kevin's disciples have been recorded, St. Berach, Founder of Termon Barry on the Shannon, and St. Mochory, grandson of the king of Britain, who lived at Glendalough, and who administered the last Sacrament to Kevin.

In 1198 Thomas was Abbott of Glendalough, as appears from a Bull issued to him by Innocent III. There is also a record of a grant by King John of the "Abbey of Glendalough" to "Thomas the Abbot," and a grant made to the archbishop and his successors, giving power to nominate the bishops of Glendalough. Count Richard (Strongbow), then Lord Lieutenant, confirmed the grant of the Abbey to the Abbot Thomas.

In 1214 the diocese of Glendalough was joined to that of Dublin, William Piro, who died that year, being the last Bishop of Glendalough. A separate bishopric appears to have been revived in 1481, when Denis White was appointed to the Sea of Glendalough by Pope Sixtus IV. He seems to have resigned in 1496-7 and was replaced by Ivo Ruffi, who was succeeded in 1500 by Francis de Corduba.

THE HISTORY OF GLENDALOUGH

The Wicklow chiefs (O'Byrnes and O'Tooles) agitated for many years for an Irish bishop of Glendalough, with little success. Some of the members of their families were archdeacons at Glendalough, one being Geoffrey O'Byrne, who held office in 1487.

Image 35-A Icon of St. Kevin

Image 35-B Traditional Icon of St. Kevin

DJ MOLONEY/J HEWES

19 POETRY

By That Lake Whose Gloomy Shore

By that Lake whose gloomy shore

    Skylark never warbles o'er

Where the cliff hangs high and steep

    Young Saint Kevin stole to sleep.

"Here, at last, " he calmly said,

    "Woman ne'er shall find my bed."

Ah! The good Saint little knew

    What the wily sex can do.

II

"Twas from Kathleen's eyes he flew,

    Eyes of most unholy blue!

She had loved him well and long

    Wished him hers, nor thought it wrong.

Wheresoe'er the Saint would fly

    Still he heard her light food nigh;

East or west where'er he turn'd

    Still her eyes before him burn'd

THE HISTORY OF GLENDALOUGH

III

On the bold cliff's bosom cast,

    Tranquil now he sleeps at last;

Dreams of heaven, nor thinks that e'er

    Woman's smiles can haunt him there.

But nor earth nor heaven is free

    From her power, if fond she be.

Even now, while calm he sleeps,

    Kathleen o'er him leans and weeps.

IV

Fearless she had track'd his feet

    To his rocky, wild retreat,

And, when morning met his view

    Her mild glances met it, too.

Ah! your Saints have cruel hearts!

    Sternly from his bed he starts,

And with rude, repulsive shock,

    Hurls her from the beetling rock.

V

Glendalough! Thy gloomy wave,

    Soon was gentle Kathleen's grave.

Soon the Saint (yet, ah! Too late),

    Felt her love and mourn'd her fate.

When he said, "Heaven rest her soul!"

    Round the lake light music stole.

And her ghost was seen to glide

    Smiling o'er the fatal tide.

        Thomas Moore

Image 38 Thomas Moore (1779-1852)

THE HISTORY OF GLENDALOUGH

Glendalough By Moonlight

Not a sound to be heard, save the roar of a stream,

    As it tumbles down glittering with spray,

The moon it is full, as the starts they shine out

    And the vale is as bright as the day.

This beautiful vale so crowded all day,

    Is now peaceful and still by night,

The lake which all day was sombre and dark,

    Is lighted up by the moon's silvery light.

A breeze is now heard, the silence it breaks,

    As it whitles, and moans, through the brake,

The leaves make a sound, 'tis all over again,

    Save the ripple it leaves on the lake.

One night spent thus in sweet Glendalough,

    Listening to the mountain streams' roar;

An impression 'twill make, as you stand by the lake,

    That will haunt your mind overmore.

Anonymous

DJ MOLONEY/J HEWES

Pangur Bán

I and Pangur Bán, my cat,
'Tis a like task we are at;
Hunting mice is his delight,
Hunting words I sit all night.

Better far than praise of men
'Tis to sit with book and pen;
Pangur bears me no ill will,
He too plies his simple skill.

'Tis a merry thing to see
At our tasks how glad are we,
When at home we sit and find
Entertainment to our mind.

Oftentimes a mouse will stray
In the hero Pangur's way;
Oftentimes my keen thought set
Takes a meaning in its net.

'Gainst the wall he sets his eye
Full and fierce and sharp and sly;
'Gainst the wall of knowledge I
All my little wisdom try.

When a mouse darts from its den,
O how glad is Pangur then!
O what gladness do I prove
When I solve the doubts I love!

So in peace our tasks we ply,
Pangur Bán, my cat, and I;
In our arts we find our bliss,
I have mine and he has his.

Practise every day had made
Pangur perfect in his trade;
I get wisdom day and night
Turning darkness into light.

Written by 9th Century Irish Monk. Translated by Frank Flower, Irish Scholar and Poet, ©1931 [poem added to work by John Hewes]

APPENDIX A WEBSITE/BOOK BIBLIOGRAPHY

WEB SITES

A History of Glendalough [mining history], http://www.mindat.org/article.php/368/A+History+of+Glendalough

Archdiocese of Dublin Overview [catholic site], http://www.dublindiocese.ie/index.php?option=com_content&task=view&id=1&Itemid=2

Favorite Monks: Kevin of Glendalough, http://www.prayerfoundation.org/favoritemonks/favorite_monks_kevin_of_glendalough.htm

Glendalough [Dochara, your Irish Friend—history, nature], http://www.dochara.com/places-to-visit/scenic-places/glendalough/

Glendalough, a Brief History and Virtual Tour by Deborah Vess, http://www.faculty.de.gcsu.edu/~dvess/ids/medieval/glendalough/glendalough.shtml

Glendalough's Monastic History [Wicklow Mountains National Park], http://www.wicklowmountainsnationalpark.ie/MonasticHistory.html

Glendalough—A Mystical Journey: An Inspirational History of St Kevin and Glendalough [DVD], http://www.brotherseamus.ie/GlenDVD.html

Google Timeline for Glendalough, http://www.google.com/search?q=glendalough+catholic+history&ie=utf-8&oe=utf-8&aq=t&rls=org.mozilla:en-

US:official&client=firefox-a#q=glendalough+history&hl=en&client=firefox-a&rls=org.mozilla:en-US:official&prmd=iv&tbs=tl:1&tbo=u&ei=z9GiTMWQAZD2tgPmvI36Bg&sa=X&oi=timeline_result&ct=title&resnum=11&sqi=2&ved=0CFEQ5wIwCg&fp=352a51ab522ec06c

Kevin of Glendalough [orthodox site],
http://orthodoxwiki.org/Kevin_of_Glendalough

Mining in Glendalough [school website],
http://www.glenrath.com/history/mining/mining.htm

St. Kevin and Surrounding Myths of the Area,
http://www.assembla.com/wiki/show/glendalough/St_Kevin_Myths

The Hollywood Stone, St Kevin's Way & Glendalough,
http://www.labyrinthireland.com/hollywood.html

The Story of Glendalough [excellent history/guide],
http://www.mountaineering.ie/documentbank/uploads/Glendalough%20-%20History%20by%20Frank%20Tracy.pdf

United Dioceses of Dublin and Glendalough (Church of Ireland) [protestant history], http://dublin.anglican.org/index.php

Vikings in Ireland [Viking Ship Museum],
http://vikingeskibsmuseet.dk/index.php?id=997&L=1

Welcome to Glendalough, Co. Wicklow,
http://www.glendalough.connect.ie/index.html

BOOKS

A Legend of Glendalough and Other Ballads, Dora Sigerson Shorter, 1919.

Church and Polity in Pre-Norman Ireland: The Case of Glendalough (Maynooth Monographs), Ailbhe Seamus Mac Shamrain, 1996

Glendalough (Gleann dá Loċ) and the seven churches of St. Kevin (Naoṁ Caoiṁġin), PJ Noonan, 1959.

Glendalough and its Ruins: A Story and A Guide, Myles V Ronan, 1970

Glendalough and St Kevin, Lennox Barrow, 1972

Glendalough Co. Wicklow National Monuments Vested in The Commissioners of Public Works: Official Historical and Descriptive Guide, HG Leask, 1963

Glendalough, Michael Hogan, 1903, 1907

Glendalough, Or, the Seven Churches, William Drennan, 1848

Glendalough, Sir John R. O'Connell, 1909

Glendalough: A Celtic Pilgrimage, Rodgers, Michael; Losack, Marcus; Morehouse Publishing, 1997.

History and Antiquities of Glendalough, Joseph Nolan, 1871

History Guide: Map Souvenir, DJ Moloney, date unknown

King O'Toole and St. Kevin: A Legend of Glendalough, found in "Legends and Stories of Ireland", Samuel Lover, 1853.

St. Kevin's Way: Hollywood to Glendalough, County Wicklow, Peter Harbison, Joss Lynan, publication date unknown

Tales and Yarns of Glendalough, Bill Fanning, 1986

Appendix B: Photo Credits

Image i:	Irish postage stamp http://commons.wikimedia.org/wiki/File:Irl_1sh_airmail.jpg Public Domain.
Image 1 :	United States Library of Congress 0994v.jpg. http://hdl.loc.gov/loc.pnp/ppmsc.09944 Public Domain.
Image 2 :	Jolanta Wawrzycka, http://www.radford.edu/eurotrails/Glendalough-gate.jpg Used with permission.
Image 3	Madeline Hill, http://medieval.ucdavis.edu/GLENDALOUGH/G5.jpg. Used with permission.
Image 4-A	Jolanta Wawrzycka, http://www.radford.edu/eurotrails/Glendalough-cathedral.jpg. Used with permission.
Image 4-B	Jolanta Wawrzycka, http://www.radford.edu/~jolanta/regular/IrelandGlendalough7.jpg. Used with permission.
Image 5-A	Jolanta Wawrzycka, http://www.radford.edu/~jolanta/regular/IrelandGlenKevin.jpg. Used with permission.
Image 5-B	IrelandGlenKevin.jpg. Jolanta Wawrzycka, http://www.radford.edu/~eurotrails/Glendalough-StKevin-Cross.jpg. Used with permission.
Image 6	Donncha O Caoimh, http://inphotos.org/glendalough-round-tower/. Used with permission.
Image 7-A	Donncha O Caoimh, http://inphotos.org/round-towerthrough-window/. Used with permission.

THE HISTORY OF GLENDALOUGH

Image 7-B	Jolanta Wawrzycka, http://www.radford.edu/~jolanta/regular/IrelandGlendalough10.jpg. Used with permission.
Image 8-A	Photo Gallery, The Glendalough Hotel, http://www.glendaloughhotel.com/photo_gallery Used with permission.
Image 8-B	Bartlett, WH, JS Coyne, et al; The Scenery and Antiquities of Ireland, 1841.
Image 9-A	Alex Mauldin, http://amauldin.smugmug.com/Travel/Dublin-April2009/7840608_VmnsV/1/509995154_uHP9r#509995154_uHP9r. Used with permission.
Image 9-B	Glendalough_monastery.jpg, Schcambo at en.wikipedia, http://commons.wikimedia.org/wiki/File:Glendalough_monastery.jpg. Used per terms of license CC 3.0.
Image 10	Jolanta Wawrzycka, http://www.radford.edu/eurotrails/Glendalough-church.jpg. Used with permission.
Image 12-A	Warrenfish, http://commons.wikimedia.org/wiki/File:Stkevinschurch2.jpg. Released to public domain.
Image 12-B	Warrenfish, http://commons.wikimedia.org/wiki/File:Saintkevinchurch.jpg. Released to public domain.
Image 13-A	Jolanta Wawrzycka, http://www.radford.edu/~eurotrails/Glendalough-StKevinKitchen4.jpg. Used with permission.

Image 13-B	Jolanta Wawrzycka, http://www.radford.edu/~eurotrails/Glendalough-StKevinKitchen3.jpg Used with permission.
Image 14	Leslie Gilmour http://www.walkinginireland.org/glendalough/gallery/pages/glendalough_021.html. Used with permission.
Image 15	Donncha O Caoimh, http://inphotos.org/glendaloughbridge/. Used with permission.
Image 17	Schcambo@en.wikipedia, http://upload.wikimedia.org/wikipedia/commons/7/7f/Glendalough_-_poor_q_-cropped.jpg. Use per license CC 3.0.
Image 18-A	Leslie Gilmour, http://www.walkinginireland.org/glendalough/ Used with permission.
Image 18-B	Donncha O Caoimh, http://inphotos.org/glendaloughlower-lake/. Used with permission.
Image 19-A	Alex Mauldin, http://amauldin.smugmug.com/Travel/Dublin-April-2009/7840608_VmnsV/1/509995154_uHP9r#509998903_ZYpD8. Used with permission.
Image 19-B	Alex Mauldin, http://amauldin.smugmug.com/Travel/Dublin-April-2009/7840608_VmnsV/1/509995154_uHP9r#509994694_CCwuU. Used with permission.
Image 20	Unknown photo of cigarette box. Public Domain.
Image 21-A	Madeline Hill, http://medieval.ucdavis.edu/GLENDALOUGH/G22.jpg. Used with permission

THE HISTORY OF GLENDALOUGH

Image 21-B	Madeline Hill, http://medieval.ucdavis.edu/GLENDALOUGH/G24.jpg. Used with permission.
Image 21-C	Madeline Hill, http://medieval.ucdavis.edu/GLENDALOUGH/G25.jpg. Used with permission.
Image 22	Madeline Hill, http://medieval.ucdavis.edu/GLENDALOUGH/G28.jpg. Used with permission.
Image 23	Anthony Toole, http://www.suite101.com/view_image.cfm/848500. Used with permission.
Image 24	Co Wicklow, Glendalough, Path to St Kevin's Bed, http://www.oldukphotos.com/graphics/Ireland%20Photos/Co%20Wicklow,%20Glendalough,%20Path%20to%20St%20Kevin%27s%20Bed.jpg. Web image used with permission.
Image 26-A	Madeline Hill, http://medieval.ucdavis.edu/GLENDALOUGH/G19.jpg. Used with permission.
Image 26-B	Alex Mauldin, http://amauldin.smugmug.com/Travel/Dublin-April-2009/7840608_VmnsV/1/509995154_uHP9r#509999464_zWmZ6. Used with permission.
Image 27	Madeline Hill, http://medieval.ucdavis.edu/GLENDALOUGH/G38.jpg. Used with permission.
Image 28-A	Madeline Hill, http://medieval.ucdavis.edu/GLENDALOUGH/G30.jpg. Used with permission.

Image 28-B	Madeline Hill, http://medieval.ucdavis.edu/GLENDALOUGH/G33.jpg. Used with permission.
Image 28-C	Madeline Hill, http://medieval.ucdavis.edu/GLENDALOUGH/G32.jpg. Used with permission.
Image 30-A	Madeline Hill, http://medieval.ucdavis.edu/GLENDALOUGH/G35.jpg. Used with permission.
Image 30-B	Madeline Hill, http://medieval.ucdavis.edu/GLENDALOUGH/G34.jpg. Used with permission.
Image 31-A	Madeline Hill, http://medieval.ucdavis.edu/GLENDALOUGH/G36.jpg. Used with permission.
Image 31-B	Madeline Hill, http://medieval.ucdavis.edu/GLENDALOUGH/G42.jpg. Used with permission.
Image 31-C	Madeline Hill, http://medieval.ucdavis.edu/GLENDALOUGH/G40.jpg. Used with permission.
Image 31-D	Madeline Hill, http://medieval.ucdavis.edu/GLENDALOUGH/G41.jpg, Used with permission.
Image 32-A	Stefan Friedhoff, http://www.stefanfriedhoff.de/Galerie/Landschaft/slides/Glenmacnass%20Waterfall,%20County%20Wicklow.html. Used with permission.
Image 32-B	Glendalough Hotel Website. http://www.glendaloughhotel.com/photo_gallery. Used with permission.

THE HISTORY OF GLENDALOUGH

Image 35-A   Sr. Aloysius McVeigh,
                   http://www.hermitage.dublindiocese.ie/images
                   /Icon_St._Kevin.jpg. Used with permission.

Image 35-B   Green, John Richard. A Short
                   History of the English People, Vol. 2.
                   London: G. Newnes, 1908. p. 894.

Image 38   Duyckinick, Evert A.
                   Portrait Gallery of Eminent Men and
                   Women in Europe and America. New
                   York: Johnson, Wilson & Company, 1873.
                   General Libraries, The University of Texas
                   at Austin,
                   http://commons.wikimedia.org/wiki/File:Tho
                   mas_Moore_2.jpg. Within the public
                   domain.

Cover: Front   Sr. Aloysius McVeigh,
                   http://www.hermitage.dublindiocese.ie/images
                   /Icon_St._Kevin.jpg. Used by
                   permission (Sepia color filter added).

Printed in Great Britain
by Amazon